Henry Edwards

A Two Months' Tour in Canada and the United States

In the Autumn of 1889

Henry Edwards

A Two Months' Tour in Canada and the United States
In the Autumn of 1889

ISBN/EAN: 9783337194529

Printed in Europe, USA, Canada, Australia, Japan

Cover: Foto ©Andreas Hilbeck / pixelio.de

More available books at **www.hansebooks.com**

A TWO MONTHS' TOUR IN

CANADA

AND

THE UNITED STATES,

IN THE AUTUMN OF 1889.

BY

SIR HENRY EDWARDS,

AUTHOR OF
' HOW TO PASS THE WINTER.'

LONDON:

CHAPMAN AND HALL, LIMITED.

1889.

A TWO MONTHS' TOUR IN

CANADA

AND

THE UNITED STATES.

We left London on Friday, 30th August, 1889, at two p.m., by London and North-Western Railway, in a comfortable front *coupé*—bright, sunny afternoon—and we saw energetic harvest operations going on all along the line, and arrived at Liverpool at 6.45. Luckily, quarters had been secured for us at North-Western Hotel. Every room was engaged, much to the annoyance and vexation of many who were obliged to

B

put up with very second-rate accommoda-
tion, and who will in future remember the
necessity of securing rooms for the night
prior to the departure of the mail steamer.

All was bustle and confusion at the hotel.
Such crowds of people, and such piles of
luggage! It is, indeed, a sight to see American ladies returning home after 'doing'
Europe—such huge boxes, five and six feet
long, and three to four feet deep, and many
of them. I was in light marching order—
two moderate-sized portmanteaus and dress-
ing-bag. The head porter of the hotel
labelled them and gave me a voucher pro-
mising safe delivery in my cabin, where I
found them when I went on board the
Cunard steamer *Etruria* at twelve o'clock.
It is, indeed, an exciting scene to see 620

passengers crowding on board ship, and the overwhelming amount of luggage taken home by the Americans. Luckily for me, I was free from anxiety, and could look on with complacency at the worry and excitement of so many hundreds stowing themselves and their worldly goods away. And then came the anxiety of getting comfortable seats at table. Luckily the captain invited me to sit at his table at the second dinner, served at seven o'clock. The 620 were all saloon passengers, and it seemed wonderful how they were all provided for. One half had breakfast at eight, lunch at twelve, and dinner at 5.30; the second, breakfast at nine, luncheon at one, and dinner at seven, and it is surprising how quickly all get settled down.

We left Liverpool at one p.m., weather fine, smooth sea, but no sunshine. We arrived at Queenstown on Sunday morning at six o'clock. Many passengers went on shore. It was a grey morning, with a cool breeze. Passengers and mails came alongside at one p.m., and we at once got under way; the sun shone, and every one settled down for the voyage.

Out of the 620 passengers, I think the odd twenty were English, all the rest Americans, and almost every one had a large cane reclining chair, enabling them to recline at full length. The whole of the upper deck was lined with these chairs on both sides, and any number of pillows, cushions, and rugs—only a small passage to pass between them, and I could not but think it looked like a vast hospital. I must confess I would never even dream of taking a trip across the Atlantic for pleasure in a popular Cunard steamer with 600 homeward-bound Americans. I certainly should prefer a less popular ship and fewer passengers. There was no getting free of the smell of cooking in the saloon, as meals were going all day long; the smoking-room was inconveniently crowded.

I had a good-sized, comfortable cabin, but it was below the saloon, and like an oven, well-nigh suffocating, and the ports had to be kept closed. However, we made a quick passage. On Monday, at twelve o'clock, we had run 457 miles; Tuesday, 461; Wednesday, 470; Thursday, 462; Friday, 501; and we arrived at the landing-stage in New York harbour at eleven o'clock on Saturday morning. We had hardly any sunshine throughout the voyage, and the latter part we had occasional fog, and the screeching fog-horn startled us at intervals, but we had comparatively a smooth sea. I came to the conclusion that a journey across the Atlantic is all very well as means to an end ; but to take a sea-trip for pleasure I infinitely prefer the Mediterranean.

I landed, and was free of the Custom House with my luggage at one o'clock, and, as New York has no charms for me, I drove direct to the Central Station—a long drive through a busy part of the city—and secured a section in the Pullman sleeping-car for Montreal. I then felt myself free for three or four hours, and drove through Broadway and round Central Park. I was much struck with the material improvement and signs of wealth in the city—all the old crude buildings cleared away, and magnificent offices, stores, and hotels erected, giving unmistakable signs of great prosperity; but the racket and noise was well-nigh unbearable. Since my last visit a new tramway has been laid through the very centre of Broadway, from end to end, and one company alone runs a car every minute throughout the day. This is in addition to the other trams and the numerous carts, waggons, and private vehicles. The great noise and confusion can be more easily imagined than described. The granite paving-stones don't add to its serenity. I dined at the Union Hotel, close to Central Station, at six o'clock, and at 7.30 started for Montreal, and passed a comparatively comfortable night in the train, and arrived at eight a.m. Sunday morning.

Sir Donald Smith kindly sent to the station for me, and on arrival gave me a hearty welcome. I found he had visitors staying with him—Lady Shrewsbury and Lady Selkirk—who were making a tour of America and Canada, simply with their two maids. They only arrived the evening before my arrival. We all met at breakfast, then went to church and had a very good service. After luncheon we devoted ourselves in admiration of the art treasures in Sir Donald's picture gallery and museum. There are very fine pictures, and a large collection of very choice, valuable Japanese bronzes, and all sorts of curios. There is a banquetting-room, in addition to the ordinary room. Our host is most hospitable; we had dinner parties every day, except Tuesday, when we all dined with Sir George and Lady Stephen.

We visited all the places of interest in and around Montreal, of which there are very many; the drive round the mountain and the commanding views from the summit are very charming, also the steamboat excursion down the Lachine Rapids. The population is 250,000, and rapidly increasing; bricks and mortar abound in all directions.

I left Montreal at 8.40 p.m. on Friday, the 13th of September. Luckily I had the drawing-room of the car appropriated to me, and found it most comfortable, and it mitigated the weariness of three nights and three days in the train. I must say the Canadian Pacific Railway is admirable in all respects—the line runs easy and smooth, the dining cars are luxurious, and the *cuisine* very good, and very superior to anything I ever met with on the Grand Trunk Railway. I cannot say the country between Montreal and Winnipeg is very picturesque.

We stopped at Sudbury, where there is a branch railway to St. Paul and Minneapolis. Sudbury is a considerable copper-mining district, and is extending rapidly. Smelting furnaces are in course of erection. We pass through hills, forests, and lakes, and on the second morning after leaving Montreal we catch glimpses of Lake Superior, and soon we are running along its precipitous shore; on the right are tree-clad mountains, mostly the green pine, and there are rocks all around. For many hours we continue along the lake, hour after hour we glide through tunnels and deep rock cuttings, over immense embankments, bridges, and viaducts, everywhere amazed at the great difficulties that had to be encountered in making the line.

We crossed the Nepigon River, famous for its trout, ran down the shore of Thunders Bay, and stopped at Port Arthur, a thousand miles from Montreal, a beautifully situated city, but quite a mushroom. Eight years since it was a mere landing-place, and now it is a flourishing town with a population of 5,000, apparently carrying on a prosperous trade, and the country around is getting rapidly cultivated. Only four miles further we came to Fort William, where there is considerable trade carried on. Long piers and wharves and a considerable amount of shipping; and the great railway grain elevator, looming above all, is a monster, holding twelve hundred thousand bushels; and everything is new—the creation of two years.

The country between Fort William and Winnipeg is a wild, broken region, with rapid rivers and lakes, and contains nothing of interest—poor soil, with poplar and small spruce-trees; and we hardly saw a living thing for very many miles, until our near approach to Winnipeg. Wolseley led his army from Fort William to Winnipeg in 1870, using the more or less connected rivers and lakes much of the way; at that time it was called Fort Garry, and there were but a few wooden huts, and now there is a handsome city, capital of the province of Manitoba, of over 35,000 people, and is growing rapidly, and has street railways, electric lights, handsome schools and colleges, a fine hospital, great flour mills and grain elevators. Since the great boom of 1880 and 1883 there has been a comparative quietness over the place, but there are now signs of revival, a few good harvests are wanted to set all alive again ; the cost of living is dear, and house-rent very high. Winnipeg has become what it always must be—the commercial focus of the North-West; situated where the forest ends and the vast prairies begin, with thousands of miles of river navigation to the North, South, and West, and railways radiating in every direction.

Winnipeg is on a broad plain, and for

many miles is as green and level as a billiard-table, not a bit of rising ground to be seen; there are numerous well-tilled farms and comfortable farmhouses, with a quantity of cattle half hidden in the grass, but there are very few trees. About six miles out of Winnipeg Sir D. Smith has a charming farm residence, replete with every comfort, which is always kept in readiness for his friends, and all repaired there, including the Ladies Shrewsbury and Selkirk: we went over the yards and saw some very choice cattle and sheep, and five buffaloes, which are most interesting objects since their almost ex-termination.

Fifty-five miles from Winnipeg is Portage la Prairie, another city of a day's growth, with grain elevators and flour mills, with busy streets and substantial houses; and eighty miles further we reach Brandon, a prosperous town of 5,000, with large grain elevators or warehouses at the station.

Leaving Brandon we reach the great Prairie Steppes leading to the Rocky Mountains, a most prolific soil : the horizon only limits the view, and as far as the eye can reach the prairie is dotted with newly made farms — here is produced in the greatest perfection the most famous wheat, known as Hard Fyfe wheat of Manitoba.

Three hundred miles from Winnipeg we passed through the famous Bell Farm, embracing 100 square miles of land, 64,000 acres, the largest arable farm in the world. It was bought of the Government at five shillings per acre. About 1500 acres are now under cultivation; the produce on an average is twenty bushels per acre. There is a church, school, hotel, flour mills, making quite a village, and neat square cottages of the labourers dot the plain.

The great wheat belt of Manitoba is about 500 miles long and 250 wide, capable of producing sixteen hundred million bushels of wheat if it were all under cultivation.

We reached Regina, the headquarters of the North-West Mounted Police, a magnificent body of men engaged in keeping the Indians in order. They are young, picked men, thoroughly drilled, and governed by strict military discipline. We then had a dull, dreary country to pass through; for over 200 miles the prairie was covered with burnt grass. We had a hot sun, and the carriages were stuffy and anything but agreeable; there was not a tree to be seen. We then pass through what is said to be a very paradise for sportsmen; the lakes become more frequent. Some are salt, some are alkaline, but most of them are clear and fresh; it is said wild geese, cranes, ducks, —a dozen varieties—snipe and curlew are found here in myriads. Prairie chickens are abundant on the high ground, and antelope are common on the hills. We have crossed the high broken country, and far away we see the Cypress Hills appearing as a deep blue line, and for want of anything else we watch these gradually rising as we draw near to them; the railway skirts their base for many miles.

At Maple Creek, a little town with exten-

c

sive yards for the shipment of cattle, some of which are driven here from Montana, feeding and fattening on the way, we see the red coats of the Mounted Police, who are looking after a large encampment of Indians near by; there are many Indians on the station platform, of high and low degree, and squaws, mostly bent on trading—a picturesque-looking lot, but very dirty withal. Leaving the station, we catch sight of their encampment—many of them in blankets of brilliant colours—hundreds of ponies feeding on the rich grasses; a line of trees in the background, seeming more beautiful because of their rarity, making, with the Cypress Hills in the distance, a picture novel and striking. In about two hours we arrived at Medicine Hut, a finely situated and rapidly growing town, a thousand miles from Lake Superior; there are extensive coal mines in the district. Some time after we approach Crowfoot Station, and we are all alive for the first view of the Rocky Mountains, yet more than a hundred miles away. Soon we see them, a glorious line of snowy peaks, seemingly an impenetrable barrier. Peak rises behind peak, then dark bands of forest that reach up to the snow-line come into view; the snow-fields and glaciers glisten in the sunlight, and the passes are seen deep in the heart of the mountains.

We have been running by the tree-lined banks of the Bow River, and crossing over we find ourselves on a plateau where stands the new city of Calgary, at the base of the Rocky Mountains, 2262 miles from

Montreal, and 3416 feet above the sea. Calgary is an infant of three years old, with a population of 2500, the most important as well as handsomest town between Brandon and Vancouver. It is charmingly situated on a hill-girt plateau; it is the centre of the trade of the great ranching country, and said to be the finest ranching country; the area is about 4,000,000 acres, well watered by streams from the Rocky Mountains. Cattle and horses graze at will all over the country, summer and winter alike. In the spring and autumn all the ranchmen join in a 'round up,' to collect and sort out the animals according to the brands of the different owners, and it is then the cowboy appears in all his glory. Calgary is growing fast into a big place. There is no gas;

electric light lights up the whole place : it is the centre of the great cattle, horse, and sheep trade, and an important station of the Mounted Police.

Our next resting-place was Banff, the station of the National Park of Canada, and we were told it was the summit of the Rocky Mountains ; but it is the summit only in an engineering sense, for the mountains still lift their white heads five to seven thousand feet above us. We arrived at five o'clock in the morning ; it was dark, but, as the dawn began to break, we soon became aware of the magnificent scenery in the heart of the Rockies, and when the sun rose and lit up the snowy peaks of the impressive mountains it was a scene never to be forgotten. The railway

company have built a grand hotel, capable
of accommodating 300 guests, in a situa-
tion commanding most lovely views.

The first thing I did when I reached the
hotel was to have a sulphur bath, for which
Banff is famous. The two principal springs
which are being utilised flow from the central
spur of Sulphur Mountain, 700 feet above the
level of Bow River. The main spring gives
at the rate of one and a half millions of
gallons daily, at a temperature of 115°; on
the left of the mountain is a cave and a large
pool of about thirty feet wide and three to
six feet deep, in which hot springs bubble,
making the atmosphere well-nigh unbearable
with the fumes of the sulphur. Some wonderful cures have been made by persons
suffering from rheumatism bathing in this

cave. A crutch hangs on the wall with this label, ' Owner has gone home.'

Banff will doubtless become celebrated by the sulphur baths, but quite independent of them the exquisite scenery and the bracing air will be attraction enough for hosts of visitors. The entire Banff Valley and adjacent mountains, amounting to 100,000 acres, have been set apart by the Dominion Government as a national park for ever ; it is twenty-four miles long and nine wide, and it embraces fifteen miles of the Bow River, of which nine miles are navigable for small steamers, six miles of the Spray River flowing through a forest. The park also contains the Devil Lake, twelve miles long and two wide, and the Vermillion Lakes ; they are deep and clear, and mountain ranges on each side, rising thousands of feet, present scenery of the greatest beauty, and just at this season it is surpassingly lovely—the bright green pine, the bright yellow of the fading poplar, and the brilliant red of the dying maple, whilst the Bow River winds through the whole, a bright blue, and the mountain range of eternal snow forming a panorama of mountains ten to eleven thousand feet high, which cannot be surpassed in beauty and grandeur.

It is, indeed, a place to remember, and I should have much liked to prolong my stay. We stayed two entire days, and were aroused at four o'clock in the morning to catch the train leaving Banff at five. The railway rejoins the Bow River, and follows it up through a forested valley. The view backward is very fine; the Vermillion Lakes are skirted, and ahead a magnificent view is had of Mount Massive, and the snow-peaks and a small glacier between Mount Hector and Goal Mountain both over 10,000 feet. Then the highest point of the railway is reached, 5300 feet above the sea; at the summit is a lake, marshy and shallow, from which trickles a stream at each end, one of which travels 2000 miles to the Atlantic, and the other 1500 to the Pacific Ocean. And now we bid adieu to Bow River. Ten miles below the summit we round the base of Mount Stephen—a stupendous mountain rising directly from the railway to a height of more than 8000 feet, holding on its shoulders, almost above our heads, a glacier whose shining green ice, 500 feet thick, is over a precipice of dizzy height; it is so near that we can imagine we hear the

crackling of the ice. The scenery is now
sublime and almost terrible; the line clings to
the mountain side on the left, and the valley
on the right rapidly deepens until the river is
seen as a gleaming thread a thousand feet
below. The train, with two powerful engines
reversed, and every break screwed to its
tightest, slides down a gradient of 1250 feet
in less than ten miles. Every now and then
we crawl over a trestle bridge two or three
hundred feet above some gorge torn out of
the mountain side by a rushing torrent.

Two hours from the summit, and 3000
feet below it, the gorge suddenly expands,
and we see before us, high up against the
sky, a jagged line of snowy peaks of new
forms and colours. A wide, deep, forest-
covered valley intervenes, holding a broad

and rapid river. This is the Columbia. The new mountains before us are the Selkirks, and we have now crossed the Rockies.

Sweeping round into the Columbia Valley we have a glorious mountain view. To the north and south, as far as the eye can reach, we have the Rockies on the one hand and the Selkirks on the other, widely differing in aspect, but each indescribably grand. Descending, we reach in a few minutes the Glacier House—a delightful hotel situated almost facing the Great Glacier, and at the foot of the grandest of all the peaks of the Selkirks—Sir Donald, an acute pyramid of naked rock, shooting up nearly 8000 feet above us. In the dark valley below we see the glacier-fed river glistening through the tree-tops, and everywhere the mountains rise in majesty and immensity beyond all comparison. **We** are now confronted by the Gold range—another grand, snow-clad series of mountains. The deep and narrow pass takes us forty miles through this range of almost vertical cliffs and lovely lakes; **and** then the Valley of Thompson River—a wide, almost treeless valley, occupied by farms and cattle ranches—and here for the first time irrigating ditches are **seen.** Flocks and horses are grazing everywhere.

We then pass through tunnel after tunnel, emerging into a narrow valley, and the rugged mountains frown upon us again, and for hours we wind along their sides, looking down upon a river. We suddenly cross the deep, black gorge of the Fraser River **on a** massive bridge of steel, seemingly constructed in midair, plunge through a tunnel, and enter the famous canyon of the Fraser. The view here changes from the grand to the terrible. Through this gorge, so deep and narrow in many places that the rays of the sun hardly enter, the black and ferocious waters of the great river force their way. We are in the heart of the cascade range, and above the walls of the canyon we occasionally see the mountain peaks gleaming against the sky. Hundreds of feet above the river is the railway, notched into the face of the cliffs, now and then crossing a great chasm by a tall viaduct, or disappearing in a tunnel through a projecting spur of rock. For hours we are deafened by the roar of waters below, and we are glad when we see the bright sunshine once more. The scene is fascinating in its terror, and we finally leave it gladly yet regretfully. At the end of the canyon the river widens out, and we see the villages of the Indians and herds of cattle. In the far distance we see Mount Baker, 14,000 feet above us.

As the valley widens out, farms and orchards become more frequent; we cross large rivers, flowing into the Fraser, and see shoals of salmon; the river was literally alive with them. I was credibly informed that the quantity of salmon taken out of the Fraser River this season was valued at three million dollars, and a gentleman, a partner in two canneries, told me himself that they had captured 30,000 salmon in one day; there was such a large quantity tinned this season they were afraid markets would be glutted and prices reduced. There are three separate runs of salmon every year. Passing through a forest of mammoth trees, some of them twelve feet in diameter and nearly three hundred feet high, we find ourselves on the tide waters of the Pacific. Following down the shore for half-an-hour, we arrived at Vancouver on Sunday afternoon, the 22nd September, the terminus of the Canadian Pacific Railway, having had nine days and nights' travel from Montreal. We took up our quarters at the Vancouver Hotel, belonging to the Canadian Pacific Company, and a most charming hotel we found it, replete with every comfort and beautifully furnished. Vancouver is the youngest town in Canada ; it was commenced four years ago, when it was a forest. It was burnt down two years ago. It is now called a city. It seems to have grown by magic. There are fine schools and four large churches, and I saw the design for a very pretty opera-house that is to be erected next spring. There is a beautiful natural park reserved. We drove through it and admired the fine trees for at least nine miles over a good road. I think there is a great future for Vancouver; it is beautifully situated, commanding charming views. Rising directly from the sea is a beautiful group of the Cascade Mountains, and there is a fine harbour, suitable for ocean steamers, and will be the highway to Japan and China. During my stay at Vancouver, I received much kind attention and hospitality from Mr. Abbot, the representative of the Canadian Pacific Railway Company.

On Wednesday, the 24th, I started with my friend, Mr. Symons, by steamer to Victoria, British Columbia, a journey of six hours. We had a delightful passage through the Gulf of Georgia, with rugged coast scenery, through islands, quite a picturesque coasting voyage, and arrived at Victoria at eight p.m., and went to Driard's Hotel, where quarters had been secured for us. I visited Victoria in 1883, when it was comparatively a mere country village. On my return now I find it a considerable commercial city, with a population of 12,000, and rapidly increasing, bricks and mortar in all directions, and a vast amount of labour employed. At night the streets are lighted by electric lamps on masts two hundred feet high, looking like so many moons. The effect is striking and light per-

D

fection. The country around is pretty; there
is a comfortable club, and a fair amount of
society. We drove out to Esquimalt, to pay
a visit to Admiral Henage on board the
Swiftsure. Unfortunately for us he was on
shore at a lawn-tennis gathering. We had
luncheon, went over the ship, the weathe
was lovely, and we enjoyed our visit. The
harbour is very pretty, and abounds with
fish.

We left Victoria for San Francisco on
board the *City of Pueblo* steamer. We resolved on taking the long sea route, having
had so much railway travelling. Most persons take the short sea route by Paget Sound
to Seattle and Tacoma; but as I visited those
places in 1883, when I was at the opening of
the Northern Pacific Railway, I was content

to take the long sea route. We had large, roomy deck cabins. The sea was calm, weather fine, but very little sunshine. We had a comfortable passage, and arrived within the Golden Gate in the beautiful harbour of San Francisco at 5.30 p.m., just fifty-four hours from the time of our leaving Victoria. We had the fog-horn going part of the day. Luckily, the mist cleared away, and we had a lovely view of the harbour, with the setting sun lighting up the fortified island of Alcatraz, and all around.

Our friends were awaiting us on shore, and drove us off to the Palace Hotel— an enormous hotel, admirably arranged; on one side the European style of paying for rooms without meals, and the other the American style, five dollars a-day, including meals.   I had capital quarters, with bath and dressing-rooms *à l'Americaine*.   The *cuisine* was excellent.   We stayed nearly a week, and did the city from end to end.   It is indeed a wonderful place, considering its youth and marvellous growth.   The streets literally swarm with people ; fine broad thoroughfares, and the most perfect cable tram-cars going in all directions, uphill and downhill, travelling as smooth as glass.   I cannot say I am as enamoured of the city as I am of the harbour. There are but few really fine houses, but there are a vast number of very pretty houses nearly all built of wood.   In one of our drives we saw a house of three storeys being removed from one avenue to another.   The country all around was parched and brown, owing to the dryness of the season, but I can imagine it is very beautiful in the spring of the year. September is the hottest month. There is a fine park of great extent, with magnificent roads. We drove through Golden Gate Park to Cliff House and Seal Rocks, covered with seals. Unfortunately, there is always a great deal of mist or fog hanging about, almost daily coming and going, in an extraordinary way. Not a day passed without misty hours, and it is only now and then we can see the beauties of the place. I was made a member of the Union Pacific Club, and when moving about the elegant and commodious rooms I could hardly realise the fact that I was so far away from Pall Mall and Piccadilly. I went to two theatres, and although I cannot say much of the performances, I must confess the theatres are much

better than we have in London. Sir
Julian and Lady Goldsmid, with two of their
daughters, arrived at the Palace Hotel, and I
had the pleasure of joining them in doing
one of the great sights of San Francisco, that
of going through ' China Town.' There are
some 30,000 to 40,000 Chinese, and they are
packed in a quarter of the city in the smallest
possible space. They have joss-houses, curio
shops, restaurants, saloons, and all kinds of
Chinese work going on. Our visit was between eight and nine in the evening, and the
narrow streets were crowded with people, and
in narrower passages, where the people were
packed almost like herrings in a barrel, the
atmosphere was far from being the purest.
We were taken to a theatre, and such a scene
I never witnessed in my life before. We

could not gain admittance at the entrance owing to its being crowded, but, by way of favour, and to oblige our guide, who was a gentleman of influence, we were passed in in single file at the back, through a very circuitous narrow passage. Mounting two or three steps, then another narrow passage, and more steps, all dimly lighted by oil lamps, at length we arrived on the platform, and it was with difficulty we could even find standing-room. And the sight before us I can never forget. The place was simply a mass of human beings welded together. Where we were we could hardly move hand or foot, but *they* were literally jammed; and thinking, as I did, of the very narrow, circuitous, wooden passage we had passed through, and the mere possibility of fire, I made my exit as quick as

I could, and was glad when I breathed fresh air again, and resolved if I ever revisited San Francisco I should give China Town a very wide berth. We passed a very pleasant morning at the wholesale fruit market, and saw very large quantities of fruit of all kinds, and we were not a little surprised at the extremely low prices, large boxes of good grapes selling, by the box, at the rate of a cent, or halfpenny, per pound. Melons, peaches, figs, strawberries, apples, pears, all in great abundance. I saw a gentleman from Los Angeles, who told me he had a vineyard of eighteen acres bearing good fruit, but they would not pay the cost of picking and carriage to market.

We left Frisco on Thursday evening, the 3rd of October, for Salt Lake City, and I must confess I did not feel very gay at the prospect of the long railway journey. We crossed the Pacific, and took the train at Oakland; this is a suburb of San Francisco, with a large population. We started at 6.30, and passed two nights and one day travelling through the State of Nevada—a great mining country and nothing picturesque; it was a wearying journey. We stopped at Reno, where a fair was held; the stock exhibit was fine; this is in close proximity to Virginia City, where there are many mines.

I was glad to leave the train on our reaching Salt Lake City on Saturday morning. I felt I wanted refreshing. We drove to the Walker House Hotel, and, having settled our quarters, we at once went off to bathe in the Great Salt Lake at Garfield Beach, eighteen miles by rail from the city, on a branch of the Union Pacific. Commodious bath-houses and a fine pavilion, accommodating 400 people, with restaurant, &c., and is very much resorted to in the bathing season. We enjoyed it immensely; the water is marvellously buoyant—it seems impossible to sink : it requires skill to keep one's body in position. The lake is 4280 feet above sea level, and so salt, no living thing exists in it. It is 100 miles long and forty miles wide, and contains twenty per cent.* of salt. That which struck me as the most extraordinary was an island on the lake, called Church Island, sixteen miles long and seven miles broad, where 10,000 sheep graze and a

* Ordinary sea water is three to seven per cent.

quantity of cattle. There are farms on the island, and several springs of the purest water. It is four miles from the shore.

We attended a fair, at which we saw a baby show. There were only twenty-nine competitors : there were five prizes. One lady exhibited twins, and got third prize.

We felt much refreshed by our salt bath, and returned, and found the City *en grande fête*, it being the annual conference of the Mormons; the place was swarming with the Mormon community from all parts. The Tabernacle was the great place of assembly. Lectures were delivered in succession through-out the day. We went morning and after-noon for a short time; the crowd was so great it was difficult to find room. The building is 250 ft. long, 150 ft. wide, and

80 ft. high; the roof is a single oval span, joined on a strong lattice work of timbers, resting on forty-six pillars of red sandstone; it will seat 13,452 persons—the largest roof in the world unsupported by columns, and built entirely of wood. It can be cleared in seven minutes; there are eight large door-ways opening outways. The organ is one of the finest, and has 3000 pipes; the acoustic properties are perfect, the voice, not very loudly delivered, being audible all over the building.

There is a Grand Temple in close prox-imity, but it is not yet finished. It was com-menced thirty-five years ago, and has already cost three-and-a-half million dollars; it is 200 ft. long and 100 ft. wide; the towers will range from 175 to 200 ft. in height; it is constructed of granite, from a solid mountain, twenty miles from the city. The Temple is near completion, and will doubtless be finished ; but Mormonism is no longer in the ascendant ; polygamy, from being open and blatant, has been reduced to the status of a common crime ; the generation of fanatics who believed in it as a divine revelation is passing away, and the new generation of Mormons, and more especially those who are themselves the children of plural marriages, have seen too many of its evils, and had too bitter an experience of its cursing and blighting effect, to desire its continuance. Of course this applies only to those who are ordinarily decent and well-intentioned ; there are still many polygamists, but they are deprived of civil rights ; they have no longer the power of voting if they have more than one wife. The Mormons have always had the ruling of the Council Chamber, but now there is every appearance of a change; the Gentiles express great confidence in carrying the elections in February next, and should they succeed, I expect there will be great changes for the better in the city and its surroundings. The climate is well-nigh perfection—never extreme heat or cold. We went to the theatre, a very fine, spacious building, and witnessed a performance of 'Youth' by Mormon amateurs; the building was crammed to overflowing. On Sunday we went to the Tabernacle; it was well-nigh impossible to get one's nose in; it was full to overflowing, morning, noon, and evening;

they have a choir of about 100 male and female singers. Every one remains seated whilst singing.

We left Salt Lake City for Denver at nine a.m. on Monday, the 7th of October, a journey of 735 miles, by the Rio Grande Railway, one of the wonders of the world.

On leaving Salt Lake City we pass through the beautiful and very productive valleys of Jordan and Utah. We saw abundance of cattle, and a large number of homesteads and neat-looking agricultural labourers' houses. On one side the Wasatch range towers up against the sky, and on the other the Oquerrh mountains have spires that seem to pierce the clouds—most charming scenery as we ascend the western slope; and we had two powerful engines attached to our train, one of which broke down before we reached the summit of the Wasatch range, and we were detained nearly three hours. There is an old saying, 'It is an ill wind that blows nobody good.' The accident to the engine and delay of our journey enabled us to stretch our legs and enjoy the grandeur of the scene ; and the three hours' delay enabled us to arrive in the early morning in grand scenery, which we should have missed in the day.

We passed a tolerably comfortable night in the train. Onward the road ascends, and arrives at Soldier Divide, the summit of Wasatch range. Descending the Divide we come upon the varied beauties of Castle Gate and Prince River Canyon. Castle Gate is at the extreme end of Prince River

Canyon, through which the railroad runs into the very heart of the range. Garden Gate is formed of two huge pillars of rock, the offshoots of the cliffs behind; they are of different heights, one measuring 500, the other 450 feet from the tracks to the top. Between the two there is only a very narrow space, and the river and the railway both run closely pressing each other. The scenery constantly changes; then comes some uninteresting country, which, owing to our accident, we passed in the night. Ascending the valley, beyond Montrose we entered the Black Canyon, and we were enraptured with the scenery; and we were more especially so knowing we should have missed it had it not been for the accident to our engine.

At times the Canyon narrows, and then

E

opens out into wide stretches, which enabled
us to see the steep crags that tower heaven-
ward two or three thousand feet.   After the
grandeur of the Black Canyon, which im-
pressed us so much, we pass into the great
valley of the Garrison River, and then the
ascent of the Continental Divide begins, and
the bewildering and sinuous defiles demand
our attention.

Looking up at the distant summit, there
is seen a narrow rim of earth, and a line
of snow-sheds, one far above the others.
These mark the line of our upward and
onward route.   Soon we forget to notice
anything but the ponderous engines mounting the steep grades, and I must confess
I breathed very freely when, emerging from
a long snow-shed, the train stopped at the

summit, and the view was replete with grandeur. To the eastward, and separated by countless summits which press their heads up at us from below, are the Sangre de Cristo range. Mount Ouray towers above all, and around it lies a sea of granite billows tumbled wildly together, holding in their embrace green valleys and sparkling streams. This is the backbone of the Rocky Mountains. On the west are the springs, brooks, and rivers that makes the Gunnison River, which empties into the Colorado and the Gulf of California, while the rivulets and streams on the east side, within a mile of the others, form the head-waters of the tributaries of the Arkansas River, which eventually forms part of the Mississippi, and empties into the Gulf of Mexico. We descend by a circuitous route, through and around the sides of the mountain, until we reach the town or city of Salida, in the Valley of the Arkans, a fine open plain, with beautiful surrounding scenery — fine houses, busy streets, large schools, and several churches. Soon after leaving Salida we came into the glories and grandeurs of the Royal Gorge—the wonders and transcendant magnificence of the Grand Canyon of the Arkansas. It is impossible for me to describe its magnificence. Engineering has wrought miracles; it would seem an impossibility to construct a railway. There was scarcely room for the river alone, and granite ledges blocked the way with their mighty bulk. These obstructions were blasted away, and a road-bed made, following the contour of the cliffs, and a very awfully grand road it is.

After entering its depth, the train moves slowly along the sides of the Arkansas, and around projecting shoulders of dark granite, deeper and deeper into the heart of the range. The way becomes a mere fissure. Far above the road the sky forms a deep blue arch of light, but in the gorge hang dark and sombre shades, which the sun's rays have never penetrated. The place is a measureless gulf, with solid walls on either side. Here the granite cliffs are a thousand feet high, smooth and unbroken, and there is a pinnacle soars upwards thrice as high. The river, sombre and swift, breaks the awful stillness with its roar. We rode through the gorge on an open

car, which is added to the train to enable
the passengers to witness the grandeur. I
must say I was glad when the perilous
journey was over. I heard it said, that
any one having the opportunity of going
over this road would be a fool not to go
over it once, but that he would be a bigger
fool to go over it twice. I can never
forget its awful grandeur.

Our next stoppage was at Florence
Station, where we saw the numerous oil
wells sending forth their thousands of barrels
of oil, and in the immediate neighbourhood
are also coal mines. We then proceeded
to Pueblo, a fine city and increasing rapidly,
a great mining district, principally lead and
silver. There are large smelting works.
We continued our journey, and stopped at

Colorado Springs, and went to the Antlers Hotel, and most comfortable we found it. Seventeen years ago this was the home of the deer, not a house existed, and now a fine, flourishing city stands, and within an hour's drive is a most lovely place called Manitou. I don't know that I ever saw a more charming, health-giving place. There are sulphur, iron, and soda springs, with thoroughly established medicinal qualities, several very fine hotels, which, I was told, are crowded during the season. The scenery around is simply lovely. I feel sure Colorado Springs will, ere long, join Manitou. It is growing rapidly, and will be the home of the wealthy. There are magnificent avenues, 120 feet wide, lined with fine trees, and many large houses, costing ten to twelve thousand pounds each. An English Doctor Solly occupies one. There is also a really fine theatre.

We left Colorado regretting we could not prolong our stay, and proceeded to Denver, and stayed at the Windsor Hotel. America is full of wonderful cities, and Denver is undoubtedly one of them. Only ten years since the population was 30,000, and it is now 130,000, and is growing hourly. The suburbs are admirably laid out on a great scale. The value of real estate is simply fabulous. There is certainly a great future for Denver.

We left Denver for Omaha. The River Platte runs through a fine agricultural country, especially Grand Island, where we saw hundreds of small houses dotted about, and fine school buildings, a thriving place. We stopped at North Platte City, and we saw the farm and residence of the celebrated Buffalo Bill : he has a large cattle ranche.

The whole district is one vast plain of rich agricultural country. At Fremont we saw one cattle store with 3,016 stalls. We arrived at Omaha, a thriving city, handsomely built, of 125,000. We drove round the suburbs and saw a number of pretty residences, then by electric tram-car we crossed the Missouri River to Castle Bluffs, a town of 40,000, a distance of seven miles, from whence we took the train for Chicago at 9.30 p.m., and passed the night in the train, and arrived at Davenport, a substantial-built town of 4,000. We then crossed the Mississippi River over a bridge three-quarters of a mile in length to Rock Island, Illinois, where we had delicious Lake Michigan trout for breakfast. We passed through thousands of acres of Indian corn ready for harvest, and forests of trees with lovely autumnal tints of brilliant colours.

We stopped at Joliet, a wide-spread, well-built city, and saw the State Prison and a very fine Court House.

We arrived at Chicago at two p.m. I won't attempt to describe this organized Babel—it beggars all description. An American said to me : ' I feel afraid every time I go to that city ; she grows so all the time, days and nights, and Sundays—the smoke of her magic expansion ascendeth for ever and ever.'

We stayed at the Palmer House Hotel ;

there were seven hundred and eighty guests staying in the hotel; it is a huge place. As we were only staying two nights we were amused seeing the crowds of extraordinary people coming and going. In 1831 Chicago was a village of twelve houses, without post route or a post office; in 1841 it was an incorporated city with a population of about 6,000. In 1870 the population was 306,000. The following year the great fire destroyed 17,500 buildings; the burnt district covered three and a half square miles. Notwithstanding this terrible set-back, Chicago is now a magnificent city and active business mart, covering, with the recently annexed district, 175 square miles, with a population of 1,100,000; the total area of her parks is more than 2,000 acres.

We left Chicago at three in the afternoon, and had sixteen hours in the train, arriving at Niagara Falls at seven o'clock in the morning. We at once proceeded to Clifton House, and, after a delicious bath and good breakfast, we revelled the whole day about the Falls. Every visit, and I have made many to Niagara Falls, increases my adoration. No place I have ever seen charms me so much. We had lovely, bright, sunny weather, and we devoted a second day, and left at nine a.m. for Toronto, and arrived in three hours, calling at Hamilton *en route*, a busy, flourishing city of 40,000, on Lake Ontario.

Toronto is the second largest city in Canada. There are fine streets and good shops. I was made a member of the New Toronto Club, which I found convenient.

Left Toronto at 8.45 a.m., and arrived at Montreal at eight p.m., stopping at Peterborough *en route*, a very pretty, thriving place. After again partaking the kind hospitality of Sir Donald and Lady Smith, I left Montreal on Thursday evening, the 24th October, for New York. Arrived in New York at seven a.m. on Friday. Met Mr. and Mrs. Kendal at Delmonico's, at luncheon. Congratulated them on their great success. Dined at the Union Club, and at eleven p.m. went on board the *Umbria*, to be ready for sailing at 6.30 a.m. on Saturday, but fog delayed us until four p.m. We had a tolerably fair passage, arriving at Liverpool on Sunday at four p.m., and I stayed at the Adelphi Hotel. Arrived in London on Monday, 4th November.

Thus, having travelled about 15,000

miles through countries which fifty years ago were as inaccessible as Central Africa is to-day, who can say that Victoria Nyanza will not be as get-at-able as the Rocky Mountains?

LONDON
Printed by STRANGEWAYS AND SONS, Tower Street, Cambridge Circus. W.C